# SUCCESSFUL NEGOTIATION
## REVISED EDITION

## EFFECTIVE "WIN-WIN" STRATEGIES AND TACTICS

Robert B. Maddux

**CRISP PUBLICATIONS, INC.**
**Los Altos, California**

# SUCCESSFUL NEGOTIATION
## REVISED EDITION

**CREDITS**
Editor: **Michael Crisp**
Designer: **Carol Harris**
Typesetting: **Interface Studio**
Cover Design: **Carol Harris**
Artwork: **Ralph Mapson**

Copyright © 1986, 1988 by Crisp Publications, Inc.
Printed in the United States of America

Crisp books are distributed in Canada by Reid Publishing, Ltd., P.O. Box 7267, Oakville, Ontario, Canada L6J 6L6.

In Australia by Career Builders, P.O. Box 1051 Springwood, Brisbane, Queensland, Australia 4127.

And in New Zealand by Career Builders, P.O. Box 571, Manurewa, New Zealand.

**Library of Congress Catalog Card Number 85-73178**
Maddux, Robert B.
Successful Negotiation
ISBN O-931961-09-2

# PREFACE

Negotiating is a fundamental personal skill that can be learned. The skill of negotiation is used regularly by people engaged in business or community activities, but often overlooked by the same people in the conduct of their daily lives. Everyone needs to know how to negotiate. For those who are fearful of the process, or too embarassed to try, this book can help.

SUCCESSFUL NEGOTIATION presents concepts that can be applied in any situation where negotiation is the method by which issues are resolved. Those who master the skill of effective negotiation will save money, save time and achieve a high degree of need satisfaction. Skilled negotiators don't have to worry about "what might have been".

SUCCESSFUL NEGOTIATION is not like most books. It has a unique "self-paced" format that encourages a reader to become personally involved. Designed to be "read with a pencil", there are abundant exercises, activities, assessments and cases that invite participation.

THIS BOOK (and the other self-improvement titles listed on page 67) can be used effectively in a number of ways. Here are some possibilities:

—Individual Study. Because the book is self-instructional, all that is needed is a quiet place, some time and a pencil. Completing the activities and exercies will provide valuable feedback, as well as practical ideas for self-improvement.

—Workshops and Seminars. This book is ideal for use during, or as pre-assigned reading prior to a workshop or seminar. With the basics in hand, the quality of participation will improve. More time can be spent practicing concept extensions and applications during the program.

—College Programs. Thanks to the format, brevity and low cost, this book is ideal for short courses and extension programs.

There are other possibilities that depend on the objectives of the user. One thing for sure, even after it has been read, this book will serve as excellent reference material which can be easily reviewed.

# TO THE READER

Congratulations on acquiring this book!

In approximately one hour you will have learned enough about the fundamentals of negotiating to repay the purchase price several times over.

You will be encouraged to complete a number of exercises that provide an opportunity to apply the concepts which are presented. You will also have a chance to do some self analysis in order to identify your negotiating strengths and weaknesses.

What you learn, and how effectively you are able to apply it depends on how carefully you read; *and* how thoughtfully you practice and apply the principles presented.

Good Luck!

Robert B. Maddux

# CONTENTS

## SOME IMPORTANT OBJECTIVES FOR THE READER

Before you begin this book, give some thought to your objectives.

Objectives give us a sense of direction; a definition of what we plan to accomplish; and a feeling of fulfillment when they are achieved.

Check the objectives on the next page that are important to you. Then when you have completed the book, review your objectives and enjoy the sense of achievement you will feel.

# WHICH OBJECTIVES DO YOU WANT TO ACHIEVE?

Once I have completed this book, I hope to:

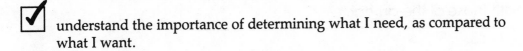 more readily identify opportunities for negotiation.

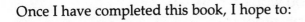 understand the importance of determining what I need, as compared to what I want.

recognize why thorough preparation **prior to** beginning a negotiation is essential.

remember the sequential nature of negotiation and why each step is important.

be able to employ a variety of negotiation strategies and tactics which will meet my needs.

confidently enter into a negotiation with a win/win philosophy.

## WHAT IS NEGOTIATION?

You are about to embark on a brief study on the principles of negotiation. You already have an interest or you wouldn't be reading this book. You probably want to learn more about negotiation or how to become more proficient as a negotiator. Let's start by comparing some of your ideas with those of the author.

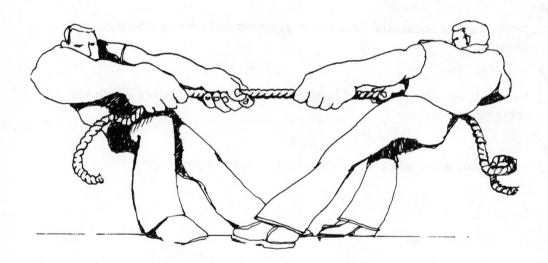

# WHAT IS NEGOTIATION?

## YOUR IDEAS

1. In the space below, write what the word "negotiation" means to you.

_____

_____

_____

_____

2. What prompts negotiation between companies, groups and/or individuals?

_____

_____

_____

_____

3. How frequently do most people negotiate?

☐ Very Rarely

☐ Almost Every Day

☐ A Few Times Each Year

NOW TURN TO THE NEXT PAGE AND COMPARE YOUR THOUGHTS WITH THOSE OF THE AUTHOR.

## COMPARE IDEAS →

Most people in the U.S. think goods have a fixed price and that it would be inappropriate to suggest bargaining for one which is lower. Yet three quarters of the world's population buy and sell merchandise without a fixed price. The value of goods is determined through negotiation between buyer and seller.

Price is not the only variable in negotiation. Other considerations include: interest rate, delivery date, size, quality, quantity, color, warranty and service.

**ANY ASPECT OF A TRANSACTION THAT IS NOT TOTALLY SATISFACTORY TO YOU, IS WORTH NEGOTIATING.**

# NEGOTIATION—SOME PRACTICAL DEFINITIONS

Following are some accepted defintions of negotiation:

1. Whenever we attempt to influence another person through an exchange of ideas, or something of material value, we are negotiating. **Negotiation is the process we use to satisfy our needs when someone else controls what we want.** Every wish we would like to fulfill, every need we feel compelled to satisfy, are potential situations for negotiation. Other terms are often applied to this process such as: bargaining, haggling, dickering, mediating or bartering.

2. Negotiation between companies, groups or individuals normally occurs **because one has something the other wants and is willing to bargain to get it.**

3. Most of us are constantly involved in negotiations to one degree or an other. Examples include: when people meet to draw up contracts; buy or sell anything; resolve differences; make mutual decisions; or agree on work plans. Even deciding where to have lunch, makes use of the negotiating process.

DANGER

There is a danger of being in the midst of negotiation without recognizing it. If this occurs, you will not be able to try to improve the outcome for yourself. If you have not thought of the transaction as a negotiation, and have not prepared, chances are the results will be less favorable for you than they might have been.

8

## IDENTIFYING OPPORTUNITIES FOR NEGOTIATION

Many people miss the opportunity to make a more favorable exchange because they fail to recognize the opportunity to negotiate. Are you missing opportunities? Test yourself on the next page.

# IDENTIFYING OPPORTUNITIES FOR NEGOTIATION

Here is a list of typical transactions. Please check those that offer an opportunity to improve your position through negotiation.

- [ ] 1. Purchasing an appliance at a department store.
- [ ] 2. Deciding with the family which movie to see.
- [ ] 3. Getting a raise in pay.
- [ ] 4. Selecting a contractor to build a new home.
- [ ] 5. Working out an effective date for an employee transfer.
- [ ] 6. Deciding on a date for the next meeting of your study group.
- [ ] 7. Agreeing on realistic project deadlines.
- [ ] 8. Buying plants for your new rose garden.
- [ ] 9. Deciding who gets to use the convertible for the weekend.
- [ ] 10. Agreeing on a change of work rules with the union.

List other negotiating situations in which you are apt to find yourself below.

_____

_____

_____

_____

ARE YOU PREPARED TO HANDLE THEM EFFECTIVELY?

**ANSWER: Give yourself a perfect score if you checked all 10 items. Everything is negotiable! Whether you pursue that reality or not is strictly up to you. It does on occasion require some courage and effort. You have to know what you want to achieve, and what you are willing to settle for. You must also know what you are willing to give up to get what you want.**

IDENTIFYING OPPORTUNITIES FOR
NEGOTIATION

## THE IMPORTANCE OF ATTITUDE TOWARD DISAGREEMENT AND CONFLICT

Successful negotiators have a positive attitude. They are able to view conflict as normal and constructive. The skills they use to resolve conflict are not "magic". They can be learned. These skills once learned, provide the courage and confidence necessary to challenge others, and initiate a positive negotiation. Understanding the skills of negotiation also sustains us when we are challenged by others.

Check your attitude toward disagreement and conflict on the next page.

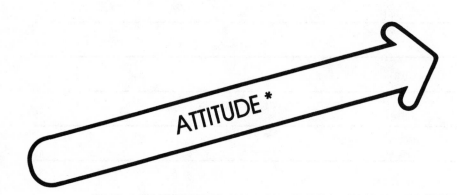

ATTITUDE *

---

* For an excellent book on attitude, order
ATTITUDE: YOUR MOST PRICELESS POSSESSION FROM PAGE 68

# MY REACTION TO DISAGREEMENT AND CONFLICT

Following are several statements about personal reactions to disagreement and conflict. Circle the number that best describes you. The higher the number, the more you agree with the statement. When you finish, total the numbers you circled and write it in the space provided.

| | Strong Agreement | | | | | Mild Agreement | | | | |
|---|---|---|---|---|---|---|---|---|---|---|
| It doesn't bother me to question a price or seek a more favorable exchange than offered. | 10 | 9 | 8 | 7 | 6 | 5 | 4 | 3 | 2 | 1 |
| I have nothing to lose in seeking a better deal if I do it in a reasonable way. | 10 | 9 | 8 | 7 | 6 | 5 | 4 | 3 | 2 | 1 |
| Conflict is a fact of life and I work hard to resolve it. | 10 | 9 | 8 | 7 | 6 | 5 | 4 | 3 | 2 | 1 |
| Conflict is positive because it makes me examine my ideas carefully. | 10 | 9 | 8 | 7 | 6 | 5 | 4 | 3 | 2 | 1 |
| In resolving conflict, I try to consider the needs of the other person. | 10 | 9 | 8 | 7 | 6 | 5 | 4 | 3 | 2 | 1 |
| Conflict often produces better solutions to problems. | 10 | 9 | 8 | 7 | 6 | 5 | 4 | 3 | 2 | 1 |
| Conflict stimulates my thinking and sharpens my judgement. | 10 | 9 | 8 | 7 | 6 | 5 | 4 | 3 | 2 | 1 |
| Working with conflict has taught me that compromise is not a sign of weakness. | 10 | 9 | 8 | 7 | 6 | 5 | 4 | 3 | 2 | 1 |
| Satisfactorily resolved, conflict often strengthens relationships. | 10 | 9 | 8 | 7 | 6 | 5 | 4 | 3 | 2 | 1 |
| Conflict is a way to test one's own point of view. | 10 | 9 | 8 | 7 | 6 | 5 | 4 | 3 | 2 | 1 |

GRAND TOTAL _____

If you scored 80 or above you have a realistic attitude toward conflict, and seem willing to work to resolve it. If you scored between 50 and 79 you appear to be dealing fairly well with conflict, but need to work toward a more positive approach.

If your score was below 50, you need to first understand why, and then work hard to learn techniques of conflict resolution. By the time you finish this book, you may wish to complete this exercise again.

## THE IMPORTANCE OF ATTITUDE IN NEGOTIATING

Our attitude is always important, and this is especially true in negotiating. ATTITUDES influence our objectives, and objectives control the way we negotiate. The way in which we negotiate determines the outcome.

Have you thought about your objectives when you negotiate? Have you considered those of the other party? Can you both win?

Go to the next page and check your thoughts with those of the author.

# DEVELOP A WIN/WIN PHILOSOPHY OF NEGOTIATION

Each party in a negotiation wants to win. Successful negotiations end with something both need. Anytime a negotiator approaches a bargaining situation with the idea, ''I must win, and really don't care about the other party'' disaster is close at hand.

The win/win concept of negotiation is not simply based on ethical considerations. The party ending a negotiation feeling he or she has been had may try to get even later.

Win/win negotiating is simply ''good business.'' When parties in an agreement are satisfied with the outcome, they will work to make it succeed, not fail. They will also be willing to work with one another in the future. Perhaps you are asking, ''How can I come out ahead in a negotiation if I permit the other party to meet their needs as well?'' The answer to this question lies in the fact that different people have different needs. How many people have exactly the same needs as you?

Think for a minute, and then turn the page to check your reasoning with that of the author.

## WIN/WIN NEGOTIATING IS POSSIBLE BECAUSE.......

Individuals, groups, organizations or nations entering negotiation with each other all have reasons to negotiate. Since these reasons are unique to the parties involved, and because each party will place different values on their wants and needs, an exchange is usually possible where it is possible for each to obtain that which is of greatest value to them at that time.

In successful negotiation, a negotiator will obtain something of greater value in exchange for something on which he or she places a lower relative value. Both parties can win. They may have wished for more, but end up satisfied.

Benjamin Franklin expressed it best when he said, "Trades would not take place unless it were advantageous to the parties concerned. Of course, it is better to strike as good a bargain as one's bargaining position admits. The worst outcome is when by overriding greed, no bargain is struck, and a trade that could have been advantageous to both parties, does not come off at all."

WIN/WIN NEGOTIATING HAS SOME DISTINCTIVE
CHARACTERISTICS. In the list below, check those you already possess.

☐   1. I have a win/win attitude.

☐   2. I am genuinely interested in the needs of the other party.

☐   3. I am flexible in my approach and willing to make some concessions
         to get what I want.

☐   4. I am cooperative.

☐   5. I understand the importance of the give/get principle in negotiating.

## THE GIVE/GET PRINCIPLE OF NEGOTIATING

For some, the word compromise has a negative meaning. For others, it describes the necessary give and take of every-day living. It is normally not possible to get something for nothing–there always seems to be a cost or concession that must be made to receive what you want. The word compromise simply means making and/or receiving concessions.

Proceed to the next page to see how the give/get principle works

# THE GIVE/GET PRINCIPLE
# OF NEGOTIATING

---

### BASIC APPROACHES TO NEGOTIATION

| PARTY A | PARTY B |
|---------|---------|

**FORMULA 1**

Give/Get                    Give/Get

Both parties are willing to give something in order to get what they want and enter the negotiation with that plan in mind. How much, and when they compromise are the details to be worked out. This formula has the most potential for success.

**FORMULA 2**

Give/Get                    Get/Give

Formula 2 also has a good chance of success because both sides understand that a good settlement requires both giving and getting. One party is willing to give providing something comes back in return. The other party will give after having received. The difficulty in this formula is that the getter may decide to see how much can be gotten without giving in return. If the getter goes too far, or waits too long to reciprocate, the giver may decide to revoke concessions previously made and the parties may reach a stalemate.

**FORMULA 3**

Get/Give                    Get/Give

In this formula, both parties come into a negotiation with the idea they will give nothing until they receive. They will stalemate quickly and remain there unless one party is willing to risk giving in order to get. If neither party budges, there is no negotiation.

---

18

**CHARACTERISTICS OF A SUCCESSFUL NEGOTIATOR**

So far you have had a chance to compare your negotiating concepts with those of the author. Now would be a good time to evaluate your personal characteristics as a negotiator.

Some people do not become good negotiators until they re-think their approach.

# CHARACTERISTICS OF A SUCCESSFUL NEGOTIATOR

This scale is based on personal characteristics necessary to successful negotiation. It can help you determine the potential you already possess and also identify areas where improvement is needed. Circle the number that best reflects where you fall on the scale. The higher the number the more the characteristic describes you. When you have finished, total the numbers circled in the space provided.

| | | | | | | | | | | |
|---|---|---|---|---|---|---|---|---|---|---|
| I am sensitive to the needs of others. | 10 | 9 | 8 | 7 | 6 | 5 | 4 | 3 | 2 | 1 |
| I will compromise to solve problems when necessary. | 10 | 9 | 8 | 7 | 6 | 5 | 4 | 3 | 2 | 1 |
| I am committed to a win/win philosophy. | 10 | 9 | 8 | 7 | 6 | 5 | 4 | 3 | 2 | 1 |
| I have a high tolerance for conflict. | 10 | 9 | 8 | 7 | 6 | 5 | 4 | 3 | 2 | 1 |
| I am willing to research and analyze issues fully. | 10 | 9 | 8 | 7 | 6 | 5 | 4 | 3 | 2 | 1 |
| Patience is one of my strong points. | 10 | 9 | 8 | 7 | 6 | 5 | 4 | 3 | 2 | 1 |
| My tolerance for stress is high. | 10 | 9 | 8 | 7 | 6 | 5 | 4 | 3 | 2 | 1 |
| I am a good listener. | 10 | 9 | 8 | 7 | 6 | 5 | 4 | 3 | 2 | 1 |
| Personal attack and ridicule do not unduly bother me. | 10 | 9 | 8 | 7 | 6 | 5 | 4 | 3 | 2 | 1 |
| I can identify bottom line issues quickly. | 10 | 9 | 8 | 7 | 6 | 5 | 4 | 3 | 2 | 1 |

GRAND TOTAL _____

If you scored 80 or above, you have characteristics of a good negotiator. You recognize what negotiating requires and seem willing to apply yourself accordingly. If you scored between 60 and 79, you should do well as a negotiator but have some characteristics that need further development. If your evaluation is below 60, you should go over the items again carefully. You may have been hard on yourself, or you may have identified some key areas on which to concentrate as you negotiate. Repeat this evaluation after you finish this book, and again after you have had practice negotiating.

You are making good progress. It is now time to look at the 6 basic steps in the negotiating process. Each step, regardless of the time it takes, is required. For this reason many people think of negotiation as almost ritualistic. Once you understand the steps and their purpose you will be able to effectively meet any negotiating challenge.

Hazel, a woman in need of a new refrigerator, will be our guide.

# THE SIX BASIC STEPS IN NEGOTIATING

STEP 1 —GETTING TO KNOW ONE ANOTHER

Negotiating is like any other social situation that has a business purpose. It moves more smoothly when the parties take a little time to get to know one another. It is helpful to assess those involved before negotiations begin. Individual backgrounds will provide an excellent guide to the level of importance placed on the issues, and the degree of expertise brought to bear on the subject. As the process starts, you should observe, listen, and learn. A good rule of thumb is to keep the beginning friendly and relaxed, yet businesslike.

Hazel is interested in buying a new refrigerator. She has studied ads in the newspapers and selected an appliance shop that seems to have good prices. She has done enough homework to know exactly what she wants and a good idea of what she should pay. On entering the store, she introduces herself to a salesperson, learns his name and tells him she would like to have someone who knows refrigerators show her different models.

| STEP 2 | STATEMENT OF GOALS AND OBJECTIVES |

Negotiating normally flows after the opening, into a general statement of goals and objectives by the involved parties. Specific issues may not be raised at this time because the parties are just beginning to explore the needs of the other. The person who speaks first on the issues may say, for example, "I would like to insure this agreement works in a way that is beneficial to everyone concerned." No terms have been suggested yet, but a positive statement has been made on behalf of an agreement being reached, which is favorable to all concerned.

The person making the opening statement should then wait for feedback from the other party to learn if they have similar goals and objectives. If there are differences, now is the time to learn them.

It is normally a good idea to make the initial statements positive and agreeable. This is no time for hostility or defensiveness. You need to build an atmosphere of cooperation and mutual trust.

> As the salesperson offers to show Hazel the available refrigerators, she comments: "I hope I can find a model I like at a fair price. I was attracted to this store because you seem to be able to make a profit and give the customer a good buy at the same time. I feel both are important."

## STEP 3 —STARTING THE PROCESS

Some negotiations are complex and have many issues to resolve. Others may only have a few. Also, individual issues may vary greatly in complexity. No one can predict the direction negotiations will take until both parties have presented the issues. There may be hidden needs neither party has raised, but these will surface as things proceed.

Often issues are bundled, so the solution to one is contingent on the solution to another. For example, "I will not agree to buy the new furnace at that price unless a free one year maintenance warranty is included."

Conversely there may be an attempt to separate issues to make them mutually exclusive. For example, in the sale of a furnished house, the seller may prefer to discuss the house and furnishings as separate negotiations. The buyer may feel they should be combined. In some negotiations, all issues are connected. No one issue is considered resolved until all have been resolved.

A skilled negotiator will study the issues closely *before* negotiations begin in order to determine where advantages lie insofar as splitting or combining issues.

Once the negotiators have reviewed the issues, they must begin dealing with them one by one. Opinions vary about whether to begin with a minor or major issue. Some feel negotiation should be started with a minor issue that has the potential of being easily resolved, because this will establish a favorable climate for additional agreements. Others feel that beginning with a major issue is best because unless it is satisfactorily resolved the others are unimportant.

> The salesperson responds to Hazel by asking what she wants in a refrigerator in terms of size, accessories and efficiency of operation. He also asks her for a price range. Hazel outlines her needs and the salesperson acknowledges they can be met by most of the manufacturers he represents. He does tell her, however, that she has selected some expensive options that will take her above her expressed price range. Hazel replies, "I don't see why they should."

24

## STEP 4 — EXPRESSIONS OF DISAGREEMENT AND CONFLICT

Once the issues have been defined, disagreement and conflict often will occur. This is natural and should be expected. Good negotiators never try to avoid this phase because they realize that this process of give and take is where successful deals are made.

Disagreement and conflict handled properly will eventually bring the negotiators together. If handled poorly, it will widen the differences. Conflict has a way of bringing out different points of view, and crystalizing the real wants and needs of the negotiators.

When presenting the issues, most negotiators will explain what they "want". It is the task of the other negotiator to find out what they "need", or will settle for. Few negotiators will get all they want, even in a successful negotiation. But good negotiators will work to get as much as possible, yet understand compromise may be necessary, and a modification of goals may be required.

This confrontation can involve stress. It is important to remember, therefore, that conflict resolution under these circumstances is *not a test of power but an opportunity to reveal what people need*. Properly understood this should lead to possible areas of agreement or compromise.

> Hazel determines the model she wants and asks the price. The salesperson says, $899.99." Hazel is shocked because by her understanding of the ads it should be no more than $750 and she says so. The salesperson points out this particular model has two features not included on the sale models. Hazel acknowledges this but still questions the added cost.

## STEP 5 — REASSESSMENT AND COMPROMISE

At some point, normally one party will move toward compromise. Statements reflecting this often begin with words like, "Suppose that...?", "What if...?", "How would you feel about...?" When these statements begin, the other negotiator should listen carefully to see if an attempt to compromise is being offered. The response should be carefully stated. Too quick an attempt to pin something down may cause the other party to withdraw because the climate may not seem conducive to giving and getting.

When responding to offers it is a good practice to restate them back. "You will sell me this vehicle, as is, for $750 less than the sticker price?" This response has at least 3 advantages:

1. The offer may be improved because the seller may get the impression your echo is a negative.

2. The seller may attempt to justify the price. This will provide opportunities for challenge.

3. An echo gives you time to think about a counter offer. Remember, however, if the other negotiator echos your offer, you should simply confirm it, not sweeten it. Your confirmation forces the other negotiator to accept it, reject it, or suggest an alternative.

---

After some discussion, Hazel says, "I just can't pay that much. I'll look elsewhere." The salesperson suggests a cheaper model but Hazel stands firm. The salesperson then says, "Could you handle $825?" Hazel replies, "$825?" The salesperson adds, "That includes transportation and connection." Hazel answers, "I can't exceed $775."

## STEP 6 —AGREEMENT IN PRINCIPLE OR SETTLEMENT

When agreement is reached, it will be necessary to affirm it. A decision about how the final settlement will be obtained is needed, especially if additional approval is required. This normally means placing the agreed terms in writing. If possible, this should be done while the parties are together so they can agree on the language. This will reduce the danger of a misunderstanding later.

Since agreement is the ultimate objective of any negotiation, it is important to determine the level of authority of the party you are negotiating with at the outset. Some sellers, for example, will negotiate in order to determine your position, and then inform you they do not have the authority to accept your terms. They then go to some unseen person who will reject the tentative ''agreement'' in order to attempt to leverage a better deal for the seller.

**WHEN YOU HAVE THE AUTHORITY TO MAKE AN AGREEMENT, ALWAYS STRIVE TO NEGOTIATE WITH A PERSON WHO HAS THE SAME LEVEL OF AUTHORITY.**

---

The salesperson responds to Hazel's offer of $775 by saying, ''I just couldn't do that but I will let you have it for $799.'' Hazel replies, ''well, OK. If that includes delivery and installation you can write up the order.''

# THE SIX BASIC STEPS IN NEGOTIATING — A REVIEW

Following is a brief summary of the six steps common to each negotiation. Keep these in mind before you engage in your next negotiation.

**STEP 1**  I plan to get to know the party with whom I will be negotiating. My objective will be to keep initial interaction friendly, relaxed and businesslike.

**STEP 2**  I expect to share my goals and objectives with the other party. At the same time I anticipate learning the goals and objectives of the other side. If possible the atmosphere during this step will be one of cooperation and mutual trust.

**STEP 3**  To start the process, specific issues will be raised. I plan to study all issues *before* the negotiations begin to determine where my advantages might lie insofar as splitting or combining issues. Once this has been done, the issues can be dealt with one by one.

**STEP 4**  Once the issues have been defined it is essential to express areas of disagreement or conflict. Only when this has been done will it be possible to resolve the differences in a way that is acceptable to both parties.

**STEP 5**  The key to any successful negotiation is when both parties reassess their positions and determine what level of compromise is acceptable. During this step I plan to remember the give-get principle covered on page 17.

**STEP 6**  The final step is when both parties affirm any agreements that have been reached. I plan to insure there is no misunderstanding later by placing the agreements in writing (when applicable), and sharing them with the other side. Mutual agreement is the ultimate objective of any negotiation.

THIS IS A GOOD TIME TO TAKE A MOMENT TO
REFLECT ON WHAT YOU HAVE READ.
COMPLETING THE EXERCISE ON THE NEXT PAGE
WILL HELP STIMULATE YOUR THINKING.

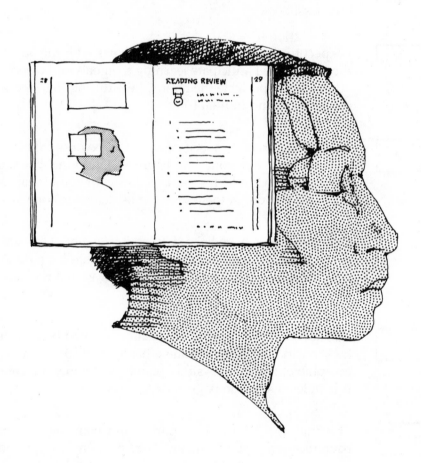

# READING REVIEW

Complete each of the following statements with the most appropriate choice. Answers at the bottom of this page.

1.  In negotiating, it is beneficial to:
    (a)  take a little time to get to know the other party.
    (b)  get down to serious business immediately.

2.  Step 2 of a negotiation gives the parties:
    (a)  a chance to challenge each others position.
    (b)  an opportunity to express objectives.

3.  Compromising in a negotiation:
    (a)  is a sign of weakness.
    (b)  may be necessary to get what you need.

4.  As issues are being clarified it sometimes:
    (a)  appears the differences are irreconcilable.
    (b)  becomes apparent that some issues are closely tied to each other.

5.  When conflict occurs in a negotiation, you should:
    (a)  work toward its constructive solution.
    (b)  go to a less controversial item.

6.  When a negotiator says, ''What if I were to install. . .?'' the:
    (a)  reassessment and compromise step has begun.
    (b)  negotiator is showing weakness.

7.  It is a good idea to:
    (a)  learn the authority of the person you are dealing with in advance.
    (b)  assume the other person's level of authority is the same as yours.

8.  The courage and confidence necessary to start a negotiation:
    (a)  are inborn.
    (b)  come with a willingness to learn skills and prepare.

ANSWERS: 1a, 2b, 3b, 4b, 5a, 6a, 7a, 8b.

IF THERE IS SOMETHING YOU WISH TO ACQUIRE
THROUGH NEGOTIATING, BE PREPARED TO
TAKE A FEW RISKS. GOOD PREPARATION WILL
HELP YOU KEEP RISKS MANAGEABLE, AND
PROVIDE YOU WITH A FEELING OF
CONFIDENCE.

THE NEXT FEW PAGES WILL HELP YOU PLAN FOR
SUCCESSFUL NEGOTIATION.

*"When schemes are laid in advance, it is
surprising how often circumstances fit in with
them."*

Sir William Osler

# PLANNING AND PREPARING FOR NEGOTIATION

> **SUCCESSFUL NEGOTIATING DOES NOT RESULT FROM CHANCE, IT COMES FROM THE SKILLFUL IMPLEMENTATION OF A WELL THOUGHT OUT PLAN.**

Whether you are negotiating with your local nursery for a few shrubs; with an international contractor for the construction of a new plant; or with your teenager for the use of the family car, planning will usually make the difference between a poor solution and one which is ideal.

## 1. WHERE TO START PLANNING

Start by thinking through your objectives.

- What do you want? What are you willing to give for it?

- What do you need? What are you willing to give for it?

- What is your timetable for giving and getting?

Once you have your objectives established, concentrate on the issues and categorize them as major or minor concerns. Do this not only for your issues, but also those you anticipate the other party will identify as theirs. Also, don't neglect issues which are common to both parties.

> ### FACTORS TO CONSIDER
> ### IN THE ANALYSIS OF THE ISSUES
>
> 1. Economic impact on the parties.
> 2. Supply and demand.
> 3. Past precedent and standard practices.
> 4. Time constraints.
> 5. Legal implications and considerations.
> 6. Long and short term advantages and disadvantages.

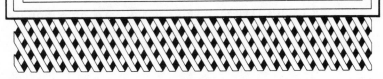

## 2. WHERE TO GET INFORMATION

Answers to most of the questions raised during your preparation are available through research. Often, all you need to know can be obtained by asking questions of others who have had similar experiences, or by doing research in readily available resources. These resources can include:

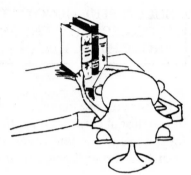

— Buyer's guides and other published product information.

— Magazine and newspaper articles.

— Instructional and educational books and/or pamphets.

— Reports by government and industrial groups.

## 3. DEVELOP A TIME PERSPECTIVE

After you are satisfied with your study of objectives and issues; and have gathered the information to support your position, decide how much time you have to devote to your effort. Estimate time factors for your opponent

as well. Time often is a pressure point which can force concessions you would prefer not to make. The same is true of the other party. If you can make time relatively unimportant, it is often possible to hold out for better terms because the other person is in a hurry to conclude the deal.

## 4. IDENTIFY SOURCES OF POWER

The relative power of the parties is another key factor to consider during your preparation. Power in this instance is not defined as the ability to force an action; but rather to influence an outcome by logic, validity, or legitimacy of a position. Following are some positive sources of power:

— PERSISTENCE—Do not concede or back off at the first sign of resistance. Give the other party time to think and consider alternatives. Then try again.

— COMPETITION—There is always competition for what you have whether it is money, ideas or products. Never forget that you always have options.

— EXPERTISE—Use what you have. You will receive more consideration from people who believe you have more knowledge, skill, or expertise than they do.

— LEGITIMACY—Give yourself and your position legitimacy by using documentation that is supportive. This often has great influence whether deserved or not.

— INVOLVEMENT—Get everyone involved. Personal involvement often will cause those participating in a negotiation to work hard to insure it doesn't fail.

— ATTITUDE—Do not relieve your tension on the other negotiator. If you need time to reduce stress, take a recess. Try to maintain a win/win attitude.

---

EVERY SUCCESSFUL NEGOTIATOR
HAS A GAME PLAN. DID YOU HAVE
ONE DURING YOUR LAST
NEGOTIATION?

---

### THE ADVANTAGES OF PLANNING

Those who do thorough preparation enter a negotiation with confidence they can achieve their goals. They know they are ready, come what may. Rewards as a result of this planning are especially high during the reassessment and compromise phase of the negotiation. This is because the value of what we want, and what we are willing to give up have been thoroughly considered. Possible points of concession have been identified, as well as those on which we are not willing to give. We can take whatever action is appropriate when the opportunity presents itself.

CASE STUDY 1

# BUYING AND SELLING

Barney wants to buy a car. He spotted a high quality used car on a dealer's lot over the weekend. He would buy it immediately if he had more cash. The dealer will only give him $1,200 on a trade for his current automobile. The car Barney wants is really great, and chances are good it will be sold in short order. Barney has planned carefully and decided he can swing the deal if he can sell his present vehicle to a private party for around $2,000. This would give him $1,500 for a down payment and $500 for accessories he wishes to add. The car is in good condition except for a couple of minor dents in the fender. The snow tires for his current car won't fit the new one, but can probably be sold and that will help. His new stereo system (installed last month) can be removed and placed in the new car.

Billie, one of Barney's coworkers, heard that Barney wants to sell his car and plans to talk to him about it. Her daughter is graduating from college in 3 months and will need a car to drive to work. Billie can only afford about $1,800 including any repairs that might be required and she needs to reserve enough money for snow tires. Her daughter has seen the car and thinks it's sporty; especially with the stereo. Billie checked the book price for the model of Barney's car, and knows the average wholesale is $1,200 and the average retail price is $1,950.

PLEASE ANSWER THE FOLLOWING QUESTIONS.

What are Barney's objectives?

_____

_____

What are Billie's objectives?

_____

_____

What are likely to be the points of conflict?

_____

_____

What power does Barney have:

_____

What power does Billie have?

_____

How important is time to Barney?

_____

How important is time to Billie?

_____

What are some possible points of compromise?

_____

_____

Now turn to page 66 to check your thoughts with those of the author.

YOUR LEVEL OF EXPECTATION HAS A DIRECT RELATIONSHIP TO WHAT YOU ACHIEVE IN A NEGOTIATION!   Studies have verified that people with high expectations usually get more favorable agreements through negotiation than those without similar levels of expectation. Lets examine this using the previous case study as an example.

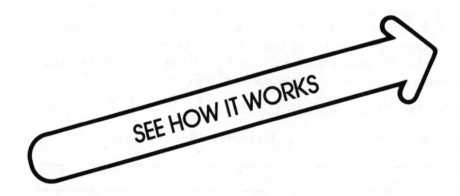

# HIGH EXPECTATIONS ARE HEALTHY

1. **IN NEGOTIATING, IF YOU SET A HIGH GOAL YOU WILL NORMALLY DO BETTER THAN A PERSON WITH LOW EXPECTATIONS.**

   If, in the case study you just examined, Billie offered Barney $1,200, she might get the car for a lower price than if she had started at $1,500. Her only risk is that Barney could get angry. If this happened she could always raise her offer a little. Suppose Billie initially offered Barney $1,200, and Barney said no but he would accept $1,850 if Billie will pay cash within 24 hours. Barney has made a concession and shown a willingness to bargain. Billie should do the same. For purpose of discussion let's say she raises her offer to $1,250. Just because Barney came down $150 is no reason Billie should go up by an equal or greater amount.

2. **SUCCESSFUL NEGOTIATORS USUALLY ARE ABLE TO MAKE CONSISTENTLY SMALLER CONCESSIONS THAN THEIR OPPONENTS.**

   After much bargaining, Barney lowered his price to $1,700 and Billie raised her offer to $1,350. At this point Barney suggests splitting the difference. Billie now has the option to hold firm, split the difference, or make a modest increase in her offer to $1,400. This may be a tough choice for Billie. Offering $1,400 is better than splitting the difference, but she might want to hold firm for the moment.

3. **ANOTHER IMPORTANT CHARACTERISTIC OF SUCCESSFUL NEGOTIATORS IS THAT THEY TEND TO BE UNPREDICTABLE AS TO HOW MUCH THEY WILL CONCEDE.**

   Barney has already made concessions and might be willing to make more. Billie will never know unless she tests his resolve.

## APPLY THE PRINCIPLE

Like any sport, negotiating skills grow when they are practiced using real life situations.

To start practicing the principles just presented, identify the reasons Tony is earning more than Joe in the case on the next page.

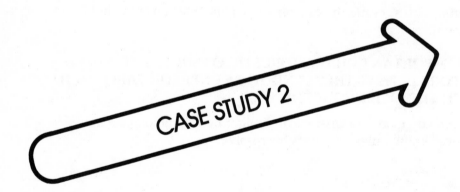

CASE STUDY 2

# WHY IS TONY EARNING MORE THAN JOE?

Joe and Tony are salesmen for the Reliance Rug Company. They are paid a standard commission based on the total of their individual sales. Both have the same level of authority to bargain with customers. They do have different attitudes toward bargaining, however, and their differences are often reflected in their income. Last year, for instance, they both sold identical amounts of comparable carpeting but Tony earned about $5,000 more than Joe. See if you can identify why this occured in the following summary of their respective negotiating practices.

Joe approaches customers as though price was their only consideration. He takes little time to discuss the virtues of the product, and in an effort to win the customers often will offer a discount before it even becomes an issue. Having set the stage for negotiating, he is anxious to close the deal quickly, and will make reductions in prices in response to any hesitation by the buyer.

Tony makes a strong initial effort to sell the buyer on the benefits of a carpet that will meet the buyer's needs. Tony does this because he feels this is of greater concern to the customer than price. Tony really expects to receive the normal retail price for what he sells, and very seldom volunteers a discount. If the customer raises the issue, Tony will negotiate to assure a sale, but any concession he makes will be small and well earned by the buyer.

List as many reasons as you can why Tony is earning more than Joe. Check your answers with those of the author on page 66.

_____

_____

_____

## LEARN NEGOTIATING STRATEGIES AND TACTICS

In the next few pages you will discover strategies and tactics to help you become an effective negotiator. Options are almost endless, and no attempt is made to cover all of them here. Those discussed are basic ploys which enjoy a good record of success.

These strategies and tactics are specialized tools you must know how to recognize, use, and defend against. They need to be learned and practiced until they become an effective part of your negotiating activities.

# NEGOTIATING STRATEGIES AND TACTICS

Negotiators soon learn that to be successful you have to give in order to get. It's an essential fundamental. The real skill is the ability to determine what to give, when to give, why to give, how much to give, and what to expect in return. To be an expert negotiator a person has to know how to maneuver so that what they *give* they can afford, and what they *get* will satisfy their needs. The techniques used to achieve this goal are referred to as strategies and tactics. *A strategy is the overall plan of action employed in a negotiation. Tactics are the step by step method used to implement the strategy.* Following are some strategies, and examples of how they can be applied.

### JANE AND BILL BUY A HOUSE

Jane and Bill decided 3 months ago to buy a new home. Their first choice is a house located in a new development, and priced $100,000 (about $10,000 above their limit). Jane thinks they should make an offer, but Bill doubts they could get the price down enough to make a difference.

Jane decided to do some research on the development anyway and learned that several of the houses, including the one they like, have been on the market almost a year. All are quality homes, but because of the economy, sales have been slow. Jane convinces Bill they have nothing to lose by making an offer. After some careful planning they make an appointment to see the salesperson for the development.

## STRATEGIES IN ACTION

42

| APPROACH | STRATEGY |
|---|---|
| Jane and Bill informed the salesperson they really like the house and might be sincerely interested at a lower price, such as $80,000. | LOWBALL—They are going for the lowest possible price and are trying to buy at what they estimate the builders cost to be. |
| The salesperson sounded shocked and said, "That's impossible, we wouldn't even consider it!" Jane and Bill anticipated this response, and asked "If you won't accept $80,000, what will you take?" | PINPOINT THE NEED—It has been established the seller will take less than the asking price but not $80,000. The task now is to pinpoint how much less than $100,000. |
| The salesperson did some figuring before he said "90,000, but you need at least $20,000 cash down." Jane and Bill had hoped for a lower counter offer, but were prepared for the $90,000 response. Bill tried another strategy by saying, "the down payment is no problem, but I understand the house next door sold for $15,000 less than the asking price. Why won't you do the same for us?" | CHALLENGE—A strategy designed to put the other party on the defensive in an effort to win some concessions. Added here to PINPOINTING to assist in determining what the seller will actually take. |

| APPROACH | STRATEGY |
|---|---|

The salesperson reacted by saying "that was a more expensive house, and we had more latitude. Perhaps, I could trim the price a bit more, say to $86,000, if you could give us your offer in writing today, along with the $20,000 deposit. Jane and Bill sensing they were close to their goal, replied, "We really do like this house, but it is still more than we want to pay. Please excuse us while we discuss ways in which we might increase our offer. Would you please reevaluate your position too?"

> DEFER—Jane and Bill take a break to allow themselves and the seller time to reevaluate their positions. Defering a decision to make this possible often proves that patience pays.

Bill and Jane returned in an hour and offered $83,000. The salesperson told them: "I called the builder while you were away to see if further concessions were possible. He gave a little, but $83,000 just won't do. However, if you would be willing to split the difference, and make it $84,500, we can make a deal, providing you sign the papers and put down your $20,000 today. Jane and Bill looked at each other and accepted with pleasure.

> SPLIT THE DIFFERENCE—Jane and Bill carefully calculated their counter offer in hopes the seller would either accept the offer or suggest SPLITTING THE DIFFERENCE. The result was a sales price at the midpoint between the seller's last offer and Jane and Bill's counter proposal.

Now that you have had the opportunity to examine some strategies and see them at work in a sample negotiation, it's time to learn others.

These are also strategies where both parties can win. In addition, they are strategies that can move you from the minor to the major leagues.

The best way to learn these strategies is to apply them.

MORE

# CHECK THE BOX ☑ IF THE STRATEGY DESCRIBED WILL FIT INTO YOUR NEGOTIATING STYLE.

☐ SALAMI

Salami is a technique used to achieve an objective a little bit at a time rather than in one giant step. This strategy is said to have been named by Mátyás Rákosis, General Secretary of the Hungarian Communist Party who explained it in this way:

"When you want to get hold of a salami which your opponents are strenuously defending, you must not grab at it. You must start by carving yourself a very thin slice. The owner of the salami will hardly notice it, or at least he will not mind very much. The next day you will carve another slice, then still another. And so, little by little, the salami will pass into your possession."

You want to buy 5 acres of land from an elderly gentleman, who for sentimental reasons does not want to sell more than 1 acre now. You are in no hurry to acquire all 5. How would you approach the old gentleman?

**CHECK YOUR RESPONSE WITH THE ONE BELOW**

APPLYING THE SALAMI STRATEGY

Offer to buy one acre now with an option to buy the other 4, 1 acre at a time over the next 4 years.

☐ FAIT ACCOMPLI

Residents of a community called Hillview, woke up one morning to discover a local developer removing the top of a peak, which was an appealing part of their view. The developer did not have a legally required permit, but once removed the hill top could not be restored. The strategy he used is called Fait Accompli. He took action to accomplish his objective risking acceptance because he did not wish to spend the necessary time, effort or expense to follow the established guidelines. In effect the developer said, "I did what I wanted to, so now what are you going to do?" This can be risky. Those who employ it must understand and accept the consequences if the strategy fails. For example, the same developer later put up a fence in violation of local ordinances. This time the citizens protested and he was required to tear down the fence and move it to a legal boundary at considerable expense.

Some examples of Fait Accompli are given below. Please indicate how you would respond to them.

| FAIT ACCOMPLI | RESPONSE |
|---|---|
| A contract was sent to you containing a provision you did not agree to and find unacceptable. | |
| You took your old vehicle to a garage to obtain a cost estimate on repairs. When you returned you found they already repaired it and presented you with a bill for $750. | |

COMPARE YOUR RESPONSES WITH THOSE ON THE NEXT PAGE

POSSIBLE RESPONSES TO FAIT ACCOMPLI: (from previous page)

1.  Use Fait Accompli yourself. Delete the unacceptable clauses from the contract and send it back.

2.  Several options including the following are possible:

    — Refuse payment.

    — Appeal to higher authority. Take it to the owner.

    — File, or threaten to file a lawsuit. If local laws or ordinances have been violated, appeal to enforcing agencies for assistance.

    — Tell others what happened to you. Document your case and let the public and others in business know of the unethical practices.

☐ STANDARD PRACTICE

"Standard practice" is a strategy used to convince others to do or not to do, something because of so called "standard practices". It often works very well because it infers it is the best way to do whatever needs to be done, and is probably a safe approach. Standard contracts are an example of this strategy. The party suggesting a standard contract assumes no one would want to change it, because it reflects what others routinely agree to under the circumstances. Often the other party will accept this fact of life, however, those who wish to test it can have good results.

A plumber who was contracted to install plumbing in a new home told his customer the payment terms were 30% when he started the job, 60% when it was half completed and 10% on completion. When the customer refused to accept the agreement, the contractor said the terms were industry standards and showed him the standard contract to prove it. The customer refused to sign. Finally the contractor agreed to 30% at the start, 30% at the half way point and 40% upon completion. This assured the customer the plumbing would be finished before the contractor could take his profit, but provided adequate funds for the plumber to carry out the project.

☐ DEADLINES

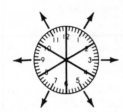

Time is critical to people and organizations. Consequently deadlines can be an effective negotiation strategy. All too often we are aware of time pressures upon ourselves, but assume the other party has plenty of time. A better assumption would be that if we have deadlines, the other party probably has them too. The more we learn about the other party's deadlines, the better we can plan our strategies. When others attempt to force us to their deadlines, we should not hesitate to test them. Most sales in retail stores that "start" on Tuesday and "end" on Friday, can be negotiated so a buyer can take advantage of them on a Monday or Saturday as well. Most hotels will extend their checkout time beyond 12 noon if you are willing to negotiate for a later time. Proposals requested by the 1st of the month are often just as acceptable on the 2nd. Deadlines are usually as demanding as we are willing to think they are. The more we know about the person, or organization that set them, the better we can evaluate what they really mean.

Before entering a negotiation, ask yourself these questions:

1. What actual deadlines and time constraints am I under? Are these self imposed or controlled by someone else?

2. Are these deadlines realistic? Can I change them?

3. What deadlines might be controlling the other side? Can I use these to my advantage?

49

Here is a dialogue between Dick Thomas, a purchasing agent and Rick Forest, an office equipment sales manager:

Mr. Thomas: The supersonic typewriters you are suggesting will meet our requirements. Can you provide 3 by next Monday for $4,500?

Mr. Forest: I am not sure we can. Because you also want the high output energizer, that puts the price for 3 over $5,000.

Mr. Thomas: That's more than our budget allows for this purchase.

Mr. Forest: Well, I'm sorry about that. To meet your price, I would have to talk to my District Manager and he is hard to reach.

What might Mr. Thomas say to get Mr. Forest to agree to supply the typewriters for $4,500, or at least to make some price concession, with minimum delay?

_____

_____

When you have completed your response, compare it with the posibilities suggested at the bottom of the page.

☐  FEINTING

Feinting gives the impression one thing is desired when the primary objective is really something else. An employee, for example, may negotiate with the boss for a promotion when the real objective is a good increase in salary. If the promotion is forthcoming so is the raise. If the promotion is not possible, a nice raise may be the consolation prize. Politicians use a variation of this strategy to test receptivity by the public to something they plan to do. Their planned action is "leaked" by a "reliable source" to test acceptability before a final decision is made. The public's response is then evaluated. If there is little opposition it is probably safe to proceed. If there is an adverse reaction, another approach can be explored.

POSSIBLE RESPONSES BY MR. THOMAS:

"Well, I'm sorry we can't make a deal. I have an appointment this afternoon with High Speed and Quickline. Both have indicated they can provide comparable equipment at a cost within our budget. The department head who wants these machines is leaving tomorrow for 2 weeks vacation. He will make his choice before he leaves today."

Successful Negotiation

## ☐ APPARENT WITHDRAWAL

Apparent withdrawal may include some deception as well as deferring and feinting. It attempts to make the other negotiator believe you have withdrawn from consideration of an issue when you really have not. Its purpose may be to ultimately get a concession or change in position. For example, the prospective buyer of a painting finds the seller unwilling to meet the price the buyer is prepared to pay. The buyer might say, "I'm sorry but I can't meet your price. You know my price so unless there is some movement on your part we can't do business." The buyer then leaves. If the buyer has made a realistic offer, the seller may decide to make a concession. If not, the buyer can always go back with a slightly higher offer. In the meantime, of course, the buyer can consider other options.

## ☐ GOOD GUY/BAD GUY

The good guy/bad guy ploy is an internationally used strategy. One member of a negotiating team takes a hard line approach while another member is friendly and easy to deal with. When the bad guy steps out for a few minutes, the good guy offers a deal that under the circumstances may seem too good to refuse. There are many versions of "bad guys". They may be lawyers, spouses, personnel representatives, accountants, tax experts, sales managers, or economists.

One danger in using this strategy is that it will be recognized for what it is. Here are some ways to deal with it if you feel it is being used on you.

— Walk out.

— Use your own bad guy.

— Tell them to drop the act and get down to business.

☐ LIMITED AUTHORITY

Limited authority is an attempt to force acceptance of a position by claiming anything else would require higher approval. Individuals who claim to have limited authority are difficult to negotiate with, because the reason they use to not meet your demands is due to someone else, or some policy or practice over which they have no control. A salesperson who cannot give more than a 5% cash discount; influence the delivery date; or accept a trade will not make concessions in those areas. Some negotiators will concede under these circumstances, while others will insist their offer be taken wherever necessary for approval or rejection. There is some risk this will terminate the negotiation, but it does give the other party a chance to gracefully reevaluate their position.

---

CAN YOU RECOGNIZE & DEFINE THE FOLLOWING?

| | YES | NO |
|---|---|---|
| SALAMI | ☐ | ☐ |
| FAIT ACCOMPLI | ☐ | ☐ |
| STANDARD PRACTICE | ☐ | ☐ |
| DEADLINES | ☐ | ☐ |
| FEINTING | ☐ | ☐ |
| APPARENT WITHDRAWAL | ☐ | ☐ |
| GOOD GUY/BAD GUY | ☐ | ☐ |
| LIMITED AUTHORITY | ☐ | ☐ |

Now that we have considered some helpful strategies, let's think about some critical mistakes negotiators sometimes make. YOU MUST MAKE EVERY EFFORT TO AVOID THEM!!

# EIGHT CRITICAL MISTAKES

Check those you intend to avoid:

☐ 1. Inadequate preparation.
   Preparation provides a good picture of your options and allows for planned flexibility at the crunch points.

☐ 2. Ignoring the give/get principle.
   Each party needs to conclude the negotiation feeling something has been gained.

☐ 3. Use of intimidating behavior.
   Research shows the tougher the tactics, the tougher the resistance. Persuasiveness not dominance makes for a more effective outcome.

☐ 4. Impatience.
   Give ideas and proposals time to work. Don't rush things, patience pays.

☐ 5. Loss of temper.
   Strong negative emotions are a deterrent to developing a cooperative environment, and creating solutions.

☐ 6. Talking too much and listening too little.
   "If you love to listen, you will gain knowledge, and if you incline your ear, you will become wise."

☐ 7. Arguing instead of influencing.
   Your position can be best explained by education, not stubborness.

☐ 8. Ignoring conflict.
   Conflict is the substance of negotiation. Learn to accept and resolve it, not avoid it.

# ACCEPTANCE TIME AND POST NEGOTIATION REVIEW

Two additional important considerations for the negotiator are; acceptance time and the post negotiation review. They are explained below.

## ACCEPTANCE TIME

As you go through the negotiating process, be ever mindful of the need for acceptance time. PEOPLE NEED TIME TO ACCEPT ANYTHING NEW OR DIFFERENT. Parties enter negotiations hoping to get what they want quickly and easily. This is not always possible. Sometimes they have made incorrect assumptions or perhaps have some misconceptions. The high price desired by the seller, or the low price hoped for by the buyer are not as easily obtained as they had anticipated. Readjustments are needed. These take time. Wishes become reality only through hard bargaining, readjustment and compromise.

## POST NEGOTIATION REVIEW

Do an analysis following each negotiation. This will help you determine reasons for your success or failure, and will be valuable information in future negotiations. Examine the strengths and weaknesses of your opponent's approach as well as your own, and file it away for reference prior to your next negotiation.

**The Negotiators Guide To Preparation** presented on pages 56 & 57 is an excellent reference with which to guide your post negotiation review.

On the next two pages you will find a NEGOTIATOR'S GUIDE TO PREPARATION. Use it both as a preparation checklist and for your post negotiation review.

USE THE CHECKLIST ON PAGES 56 AND 57. IT WON'T TAKE LONG FOR A MINOR NEGOTIATION, AND YOU CAN'T AFFORD TO MISS ANYTHING IN A MAJOR ONE.

# NEGOTIATOR'S GUIDE TO PREPARATION

☐ 1. **DEFINE GOALS AND OBJECTIVES**

— Exactly what do I want from this negotiation?

— What do I have to get to meet my needs?

— What am I willing to give up to get what I want?

— What are my time and economic requirements for this negotiation?

☐ 2. **CLARIFY THE ISSUES**

— What are the issues as I see them?

— What is the supporting framework for my position?

— How will I present it to the other party?

— What are the issues as seen by the other party?

— How will they support their position?

— What appear to be the significant differences in the way the parties view the issues?

☐ 3. **GATHER INFORMATION**

— Who will I be negotiating with and what do I know about them? How do they approach a negotiation? What are their ego needs?

— When and where will the negotiation take place? What advantages or disadvantages do the alternatives have for me?...for the other party?

— What are the economic, political and human implications of the issues?

— What personal power do I have that can be used constructively in this negotiation?

☐ 4. **HUMANIZE AND SET THE CLIMATE**

    — How can I best establish rapport with the other party?

    — How can I establish a win/win climate?

☐ 5. **PREPARE FOR CONFLICT**

    — What will be the major points of conflict?

    — How will I determine what the other party needs as compared to what they want?

☐ 6. **COMPROMISE/RESOLUTION OF THE ISSUES**

    — How will I attempt to resolve conflict? How will I respond to the other parties attempts to resolve conflict?

    — What concessions am I prepared to make? Under what conditions?

    — What do I expect in return for my concessions?

☐ 7. **AGREEMENT AND CONFIRMATION**

    — How formal must it be?

    — What approval process will be required? How long will it take?

    — What implementation steps will be needed?

## MEASURE YOUR PROGRESS

It is time now to review the progress you have made. There are 20 statements on the following page. They are either true or false. Each correct answer is worth 5 points. If your score was 80 or better you have the knowledge necessary to become an excellent negotiator. If your score is below 80, re-read this book and retake the test. Remember good negotiators are "made not born".

# READING REVIEW

For each statement below, put a check under true or false.

*True*   *False*

_____ _____   1.  Negotiating skills can be learned but they require consistent practice

_____ _____   2.  Good negotiators are willing to research and analyze issues carefully.

_____ _____   3.  Negotiating is one area in which patience is not a virtue.

_____ _____   4.  Advance planning is not possible in negotiating.

_____ _____   5.  Successful negotiators stress winning at any cost.

_____ _____   6.  Too much advance preparation reduces your flexibility.

_____ _____   7.  Compromise is a tool used by weak negotiators to save face.

_____ _____   8.  Conflict is an important part of any negotiation.

_____ _____   9.  People need to be given time to accept changes and new ideas.

_____ _____   10.  Always do a ''post negotiation analysis'' to improve your learning from experience.

_____ _____   11.  Most of the information we need prior to a negotiation can be obtained by asking questions and doing some basic research.

_____ _____   12.  The more authority you have, the better when negotiating.

_____ _____   13.  Your objectives for every negotiation should be well thought out.

_____ _____   14.  Negotiators should be well versed in the techniques of conflict resolution.

_____ _____   15.  Your expectation level has a direct relationship to what you achieve in a negotiation.

_____ _____   16.  Anytime we attempt to influence another person through an exchange of ideas, or something of material value, we are negotiating.

_____ _____   17.  It is possible for both parties to win in a negotiation because everyone has different needs and values.

_____ _____   18.  You must give to get is a basic rule of negotiating.

_____ _____   19.  Competition for what you have whether it is money, ideas or products is a source of power.

_____ _____   20.  *Successful Negotiation* is a great start to build negotiating skills but it should be followed with additional reading, training and practice.

TOTAL CORRECT _____ (ANSWERS ON PAGE 61)

CHECK YOUR ANSWERS TO THE REVIEW
QUESTIONS. IF YOU MISSED ANY, IT WILL BE
HELPFUL TO REVIEW THE SECTIONS OF THE
BOOK IN WHICH THEY WERE COVERED.

ANSWERS TO READING REVIEW

*ANSWERS TO EXERCISE ON PAGE 59:*

1. True    Practice makes perfect.

2. True    An essential effort.

3. False    Patience and fortitude are musts.

4. False    Planning is one of the secrets of success.

5. False    Successful negotiators believe it is a win/win process.

6. False    Advance preparation enables flexibility.

7. False    Compromise is a basic method of conflict resolution.

8. True    When there is no disagreement, there is no need to negotiate.

9. True    Acceptance time should be an integral part of the plan.

10. True    Learn from experience.

11. True

12. False    Too much authority can lead to a settlement before all the options have been tested.

13. True    You must know what you want to achieve.

14. True

15. True    Those who expect little, achieve little.

16. True    This is an ideal result of negotiation.

17. True

18. True

19. True    An especially great power source when linked with patience.

20. True    Review it prior to any negotiation.

## MAKE PLANS NOW TO APPLY WHAT YOU HAVE LEARNED!

REFLECT FOR A MOMENT ON WHAT
YOU HAVE BEEN LEARNING—THEN
DEVELOP A PERSONAL ACTION PLAN
USING THE FOLLOWING GUIDE TO
APPLY WHAT YOU HAVE LEARNED.

Think over the material you have read; the self-analysis questionnaires, the
case studies and the reinforcement exercises. What did you learn about
negotiating? What did you learn about yourself? How can you apply what
you have learned to your personal life? Your business life? Your community
life? Make a commitment to beome a better negotiator. Design a personal
action plan that will help you accomplish this goal.

# MY PERSONAL ACTION PLAN

_____
Name and Date

1. My current negotiating skills are effective in the following areas:

   _____

   _____

   _____

2. I need to improve my negotiating skills in the following areas:

   _____

   _____

   _____

3. My negotiating skills improvement goals are as follows: (Be sure your goals are specific, attainable and measureable.)

   _____

   _____

   _____

4. These people and resources can help me accomplish my goals:

   _____

   _____

   _____

5. These are my action steps and time table to accomplish my goals:

   _____

   _____

## VOLUNTARY CONTRACT

Sometimes our desire to improve personal skills can be assisted by making a contract with a friend, spouse, or supervisor. If you believe a contract would help you, use the form on the following page. If the contract provided doesn't suit you, negotiate one that does.

CONSIDER A VOLUNTARY CONTRACT

# CONTRACT*

I, _____ , hereby agree

*(Your name)*

to meet with the individual designated below within

thirty days to discuss my progress toward incorporating the

techniques and ideas of negotiation presented in this program.

The purpose of this meeting will be to *review* areas of strength

and establish action steps for areas where improvement may

still be required.

_____

*Signature*

I agree to meet with the above person on

_____

*Month*                          *Date*                          *Time*

at the following location.

_____


_____

*Signature*

*This agreement can be initiated either by you or your superior. Its purpose is to motivate you to incorporate concepts and techniques of this program into your daily activities. It also provides a degree of accountability between you and a person you respect.

# AUTHOR'S ANSWERS TO THE CASE STUDIES

**CASE 1 (page 35)**

**BUYING AND SELLING**

Barney's objective is to sell his existing vehicle for enough to finance a new one. He wants $2,000 but he knows the dealer will only give him $1,200. He needs $1,500 to finance the new one. Chances are good he will be satisfied with $1,500.

Billie's objective is to buy a good used car for her daughter for under $1,800. She wants to keep a small reserve for repairs and enough to buy some snow tires.

Points of conflict between Barney and Billie are most likely to be price and equipment to be included with the car. Barney's power comes from having a car in good repair, that Billie's daughter likes, in Billie's price range. Additional power comes from the fact that Barney's car will also be attractive to others.

Billie has power because there are many used cars in her price range to choose from. Billie also has power because time is important to Barney, and Billie has 3 months to shop.

Possible points of compromise include the price, whether or not the snow tires and/or stereo are included, and what can be done about the minor dents.

Many variations are possible and both parties should think them through before negotiations begin.

**CASE 2 (page 39)**

**WHY IS TONY EARNING MORE THAN JOE?**

Tony sells the customer on the product first by showing how it will fulfill the customer's needs. Once the buyer has this assurance, price may become less important. For the buyer to select another product or vendor, might involve risking some need satisfaction. If Tony does not suggest a discount, many buyers will pay retail price. He always has price flexibility to fall back on. Consequently, Tony's high expectations pay off. Tony makes the buyer work for concessions. These cost Tony little but make buyers feel good when they win one. Tony earns more because he sells at least as much as Joe and at a consistently higher price.

# THE FIFTY-MINUTE SERIES

| Quantity | Title | Code # | Price | Amount |
|---|---|---|---|---|
| | The Fifty-Minute Supervisor—*2nd Edition* | 58-0 | $6.95 | |
| | Effective Performance Appraisals—*Revised* | 11-4 | $6.95 | |
| | Successful Negotiation—*Revised* | 09-2 | $6.95 | |
| | Quality Interviewing—*Revised* | 13-0 | $6.95 | |
| | Team Building: An Exercise in Leadership—*Revised* | 16-5 | $7.95 | |
| | Performance Contracts: The Key To Job Success—*Revised* | 12-2 | $6.95 | |
| | Personal Time Management | 22-X | $6.95 | |
| | Effective Presentation Skills | 24-6 | $6.95 | |
| | Better Business Writing | 25-4 | $6.95 | |
| | Quality Customer Service | 17-3 | $6.95 | |
| | Telephone Courtesy & Customer Service | 18-1 | $6.95 | |
| | Restaurant Server's Guide To Quality Service—*Revised* | 08-4 | $6.95 | |
| | Sales Training Basics—*Revised* | 02-5 | $6.95 | |
| | Personal Counseling—*Revised* | 14-9 | $6.95 | |
| | Balancing Home & Career | 10-6 | $6.95 | |
| | Mental Fitness: A Guide To Emotional Health | 15-7 | $6.95 | |
| | Attitude: Your Most Priceless Possession | 21-1 | $6.95 | |
| | Preventing Job Burnout | 23-8 | $6.95 | |
| | Successful Self-Management | 26-2 | $6.95 | |
| | Personal Financial Fitness | 20-3 | $7.95 | |
| | Job Performance and Chemical Dependency | 27-0 | $7.95 | |
| | Career Discovery—*Revised* | 07-6 | $6.95 | |
| | Study Skills Strategies—*Revised* | 05-X | $6.95 | |
| | I Got The Job!—*Revised* | 59-9 | $6.95 | |
| | Effective Meetings Skills | 33-5 | $7.95 | |
| | The Business of Listening | 34-3 | $6.95 | |
| | Professional Sales Training | 42-4 | $7.95 | |
| | Customer Satisfaction: The Other Half of Your Job | 57-2 | $7.95 | |
| | Managing Disagreement Constructively | 41-6 | $7.95 | |
| | Professional Excellence for Secretaries | 52-1 | $6.95 | |
| | Starting A Small Business: A Resource Guide | 44-0 | $7.95 | |
| | Developing Positive Assertiveness | 38-6 | $6.95 | |
| | Writing Fitness-Practical Exercises for Better Business Writing | 35-1 | $7.95 | |
| | An Honest Day's Work: Motivating Employees to Give Their Best | 39-4 | $6.95 | |
| | Marketing Your Consulting & Professional Services | 40-8 | $7.95 | |
| | Time Management On The Telephone | 53-X | $6.95 | |
| | Training Managers to Train | 43-2 | $7.95 | |
| | New Employee Orientation | 46-7 | $6.95 | |
| | The Art of Communicating: Achieving Impact in Business | 45-9 | $7.95 | |
| | Technical Presentation Skills | 55-6 | $7.95 | |
| | Plan B: Protecting Your Career from the Winds of Change | 48-3 | $7.95 | |
| | A Guide To Affirmative Action | 54-8 | $7.95 | |
| | Memory Skills in Business | 56-4 | $6.95 | |

**(Continued on next page)**

# THE FIFTY-MINUTE SERIES
## (Continued)

☐ Send volume discount information.

☐ Add my name to CPI's mailing list.

| | Amount |
|---|---|
| Total  (from other side) | |
| Shipping ($1.50 first book, $.50 per title thereafter) | |
| California Residents add 7% tax | |
| **Total** | |

Ship to: _____

_____

_____

_____

Phone number: _____

Bill to: _____

_____

_____

_____

P.O. # _____

---

**All orders except those with a P.O.# must be prepaid.
Call (415) 949-4888 for more information.**

---

## BUSINESS REPLY
FIRST CLASS          PERMIT NO. 884          LOS ALTOS, CA

POSTAGE WILL BE PAID BY ADDRESSEE

**Crisp Publications, Inc.**
95 First Street
Los Altos, CA 94022

NO POSTAGE
NECESSARY
IF MAILED
IN THE
UNITED STATES